The Power

of

Affirmations

1,000 Positive Affirmations

By
Louise Stapely

First published January 2014

ISBN-13: 978-1495221415
ISBN-10: 1495221415

Books by Louise Stapely (LOA in Action Series)

30 Law of Attraction Practical Exercises
The Power of Affirmations & the Secret to Their Success
33 Guided Visualization Scripts to Create the Life of Your Dreams

~ Contents ~

Introduction.. 5

1. The Purpose of Affirmations.. 7

2. How to Create Effective Affirmations................................. 9

3. How to Tell if an Affirmation Will Work.......................... 14

4. How Often to Recite Affirmations.................................. 17

5. The Best Way to Recite Affirmations.............................. 19

6. Common Challenges in Using Affirmations.................... 24

7. Conclusion: Use Affirmations With Care....................... 27

8. Affirmations for the Physical Body............................... 29

    - Weight Loss.. 29

    - Anti Aging.. 33

    - Weight Gain... 35

    - Healthy Hair & Nails................................... 37

    - Exercise.. 39

    - Health.. 41

9. Affirmations for Wealth & Success.............................. 44

    - Money.. 44

    - Career.. 47

- Success.. 49

- Abundance... 52

10. Affirmations for Love & Relationships..................... 54

- Love.. 54

- Friendship... 57

- Romance.. 60

- Family.. 62

- Children/Parent.. 64

- Marriage.. 67

11. Affirmations for Self Image....................................... 70

- Self Esteem... 70

- Confidence... 72

- Strength... 74

- Wisdom.. 76

- Attitude.. 78

- Memory.. 80

12. Affirmations for Peace & Harmony........................... 82

- Forgiveness.. 82

- Happiness... 85

- Faith... 88

- Peace.. 90

- Safety... 93

- Trust... 95

- Life... 97

~ Introduction ~

While affirmations are one of the most popular personal development tools, they can also be one of the least effective, simply because some people are not aware of the correct way to utilize them.

One of the most common misconceptions about affirmations is that they act as "magical incantations" that will transform specific aspects of your life overnight. Would you like to be financially abundant? Repeat an affirmation that you are a millionaire, and *poof!* you are wealthy. Want to regain your youthful figure? Keep saying that you weigh _____ pounds and certainly your body will transform before your very eyes.

Unfortunately, you and countless others have learned that is just isn't that simple.

Most of the "ready-made" affirmation examples you see in books and online use strong wording and make bold claims that differ dramatically from your current experience:

- *I am healthy, wealthy and happy.*
- *I have boundless energy and vitality.*
- *I am rich beyond my wildest dreams.*
- *I am physically fit, strong and confident.*
- *I am in a healthy, harmonious relationship.*

The problem is that your subconscious mind will resist statements like these if they aren't true. They don't fit into your current belief system, therefore you cannot internalize them – not as they currently are, anyway. That's why simply saying that you are wealthy won't make you wealthy, and why saying you weigh _____ pounds won't make you lose weight.

So, does that mean affirmations don't work?

Not at all! They work beautifully and are very powerful – if used in the correct way. I am going to walk you through an easy process for creating powerful affirmations that DO work, and work quickly.

First, let's explore the true purpose of affirmations.

~ Chapter One ~
The Purpose of Affirmations

Believe it or not, the words in an affirmation have no power to change anything in your life. Like I said, affirmations are not magical incantations, and you may be surprised to learn that the purpose of an affirmation is NOT to change anything outside of yourself but to change the way you FEEL about a specific area of your life.

When you feel differently about something, you will start to think and believe differently about it. And when you think, feel and believe differently, you will take different actions and different, more positive experiences will manifest in your life.

Many people don't grasp the importance of this concept, so they create affirmations that focus more on their outer conditions rather than how they actually feel. As a result, their beliefs don't change, their actions don't change, and unfortunately their current circumstances remain as they are.

With this in mind, think back to the examples I mentioned in the introduction at the beginning of this book.

- *I am healthy, wealthy and happy.*
- *I have boundless energy and vitality.*
- *I am rich beyond my wildest dreams.*
- *I am physically fit, strong and confident.*
- *I am in a healthy, harmonious relationship.*

When you repeat them, do they make you feel differently about money, health or relationships? More likely, you don't feel much of anything at all when you read them. That's because they don't get to the heart of what you really want, which is to FEEL differently about those areas of your life.

Take a moment right now and jot down a few key words about how you would like to feel regarding the main areas of your life:

- Wealth & Abundance
- Health and Well-Being
- Happiness & Confidence
- Love & Relationships
- Success & Career

Do you yearn for a greater sense of peace, happiness, security, freedom, fun, passion, ease, or meaning? If you could create anything you wanted in these areas, what would you create? What is important to you? Which negative habits and qualities would you like to release?

Using your notes, you can begin to develop affirmations that are right for you; ones that resonate with your heart and make you FEEL better. First, let us take a look at how to create effective affirmations.

~ Chapter Two ~
How to Create Effective Affirmations

N ow that you have a clearer picture of specific goals in the key areas of your life, it's time to explore just what makes an affirmation effective.

Read the following affirmation and consider how it makes you feel:

- *I achieve my goals quickly and easily.*

If you are like most people, you probably feel some resistance to that statement. Most of us do not achieve goals quickly or easily – more often it's a long, strenuous journey to success. Even if you didn't experience a feeling of resistance to the affirmation, you may have felt detached or impassive when you read it, like it just doesn't have any meaning for you.

Based on the concepts we've covered so far, would you say that this is an effective affirmation?

Perhaps if a person had experience in achieving goals quickly and easily, they might be open to an affirmation like that; but for the majority of "average" people the answer would be no.

How about this alternative wording:

- *I am capable of achieving my goals quickly and easily.*

That one feels a little better, doesn't it? You aren't saying that you always achieve your goals quickly and easily, but you are affirming you are at least <u>capable</u> of doing so. This affirmation may feel a little better, but it can still be improved.

- *I am eager to achieve my goals quickly and easily.*

That one feels better; a little more upbeat and inspiring, right? Maybe it even triggers a little glimmer of hope that it's possible to achieve your goals quickly and easily? How about this one:

- *I am ready to achieve my goals easily and quickly.*

Notice one important thing about these examples – all I am doing is inserting **emotionally-charged** words into the original affirmation! Capable, eager, ready . . . these words simply trigger your emotions so that the statement makes you feel better about your goals.

Do you think that feeling better about your goals will bump up your level of motivation and determination? Do you think that being eager and ready to move forward might inspire more focused action and persistent effort over time? Absolutely!

Remember, the true power of an affirmation is that it makes you feel differently, form better beliefs, and take more productive actions. Now you can see how this works in our examples.

Next we'll go over the exact steps you should take when writing your own powerful affirmations:

Step One: Identify the Goal

First, you need to be very clear about what you want. Not the outer goal; but the inner goal of how you want to FEEL. Focus on the essence of the feeling you are aiming for. For example, you want to feel confident, strong, empowered, happy, uplifted, free, inspired, loved, proud, secure, and so on.

If you were creating an affirmation to help you lose weight, your goal would probably be to feel proud of your body, light, happy, confident, or craving-free. Ideally you will want to focus on just ONE essence per affirmation rather than trying to cram a bunch of different goals into one.

Let's say that your main goal is to overcome feelings of self-loathing and start loving your body. The essence you are going for is self-acceptance. You could call it different names but it really comes down to being able to accept your body rather than hating it.

Step Two: Lay the Foundation

Now create the basic affirmation, which is simply the new "truth" you wish to experience. Using the weight loss example above, your new affirmation might be:

- *I completely love and accept my body.*

But remember, if you don't feel so good about your body, that statement is going to trigger a strong feeling of resistance, disbelief, and maybe even anger or disgust. You just won't believe it's true because it ISN'T true (yet).

That's okay – we're just laying the foundation before we move on to the next step.

Step Three: Soften Rough Edges

Right now your affirmation doesn't feel good to you – it just brings up some unpleasant thoughts and feelings and does nothing to shift your beliefs about your body. However, there are many ways we can "soften" it a bit and make it feel better. For example, adding the word **"choose"**.

- *I choose to love and accept my body.*

Adding that little word helped, didn't it? But some people still might struggle with the affirmation even in its altered form. How about adding **"okay"**:

- *It's okay to love and accept my body.*

Ah, that one is better! You aren't saying that you DO love and accept your body; just that it's <u>okay</u> to do so. Even though we're taking a roundabout route to the main goal, you can still feel a stronger sense of acceptance about your body, right? If you were to recite this affirmation regularly for a few days, do you think you would start to feel more accepting of your body? Probably so!

Another way to soften the rough edges is to add an element of **"will"**:

- *I am willing to love and accept my body.*

If that one still feels a bit too unbelievable, you could add **"learn"**:

- *I am willing to learn how to love and accept my body. (or)*
- *I am learning how to love and accept my body.*

Softening the edges just means choosing words that are a bit more relaxed so that you have an easier time believing in the concept. Most often this is a temporary measure because after saying the softer version for a few days to a few weeks, you will be able to step up to the stronger version.

For example, starting with, *"It's okay to love and accept my body"* can easily lead to *"I choose to love and accept my body,"* and then straight to *"I completely love and accept my body."* This is an effective way to gradually improve your beliefs and feelings on any subject.

~ Chapter Three ~
How to Tell if an Affirmation Will Work

You can probably guess what comes next. You can tell that an affirmation will work by the way it makes you feel when you say it. If it makes you feel good in any way (positive, uplifted, inspired, motivated, enthusiastic, optimistic) then it's going to be effective.

If it makes you feel negative in any way, then it's not going to work until you tweak it further. While reciting your affirmations, notice if you experience any of these feelings:

Doubt
If you feel a twinge of doubt or disbelief when you say an affirmation, it's not going to be effective because that's a sure sign the affirmation conflicts with your existing belief structure. By nature, your mind is programmed to resist anything that conflicts with your beliefs.

Discomfort
You may also feel a sense of discomfort when saying an affirmation; this usually happens when you feel as if you are "lying". Again, this is because your existing beliefs directly contradict the affirmation and so your subconscious cannot accept it as true.

Anxiety
If you feel anxious when you state an affirmation, there could be two things going on. First, you may feel more intense discomfort as described above; a sense that you are "lying" and you don't feel good about it.

Another possibility is that the goal itself makes you feel anxious. For example, saying an affirmation like, "I am a millionaire" might create a sense of anxiety if you have fears about having too much money.

If you do not believe you deserve to be financially successful, or if you worry that people would constantly bother you for money . . . these fears might make you resist the achievement of your goal. This resistance will make you feel anxious and uncomfortable.

In that case, the only way to get rid of the anxiety is to work through the fear and release it. For example, change:

"I am a millionaire" to *"It's ok to have money"*

Pessimism

Pessimism is also an indication that you don't believe the affirmation to be true. It is a strong, negative feeling and may also indicate other issues that need to be addressed.

For example, you may have an existing belief that you'll never succeed at anything. Not surprisingly, reciting an affirmation that conflicts with this belief may make you feel annoyed or even downright angry, which can come through as pessimism.

In that case, you would need to improve your limiting belief before the affirmation would work for you. Interestingly, you could use another affirmation to start breaking down that inner resistance to success! Then as you start to feel more optimistic about success, you would find that other affirmations are easier to internalize.

Neutrality

It's also possible that you will feel nothing at all when reciting an affirmation. This is usually an indication that the affirmation is not targeted enough regarding what you really want.

For example, you may think that you need to build up your level of self-acceptance, when in fact you often feel self-conscious and would benefit more from an affirmation geared toward confidence and empowerment. Or you may think you just want a better job, but deep inside you are really craving a stronger sense of security and stability.

These may seem like small differences, but remember that affirmations are meant to connect you with the specific "essence" of something you want, and if you don't use the right words you will end up missing the target and not getting the results you hoped for.

The good news is that even when you can tell an affirmation isn't going to be effective, you can still keep tweaking it as much as you like until it becomes more believable to you. And you won't have to waste days or weeks trying to figure out whether it will work for you; you can tell within moments after saying it.

If it doesn't trigger some kind of positive feeling within you, you are not done tweaking yet.

~ Chapter Four ~
How Often to Recite Affirmations

In order to be effective, affirmations really need to be recited MANY times each day. Most people say affirmations perhaps once or twice a day, and they don't realize that they aren't being nearly proactive enough to create substantial change.

Remember that an affirmation is supposed to shift how you think, feel and believe about a certain subject. If you put forth tiny, gradual efforts, you will receive tiny, gradual results. Big, powerful efforts yield big, powerful results!

I always recommend that people sleep, eat, and LIVE their affirmation. Say it hundreds of times a day. Make a song out of it and sing it while you're driving, cleaning, walking the dog, shopping, working, or doing anything else. Make it a constant fixture in your mental processes.

Say it a dozen or more times when you first wake up in the morning, a dozen or more times before you go to sleep at night, and MANY dozens of times throughout the entire day.

Don't worry – you won't have to do this forever; just until the new "truth" starts to sink into your mind and take root there. This could take anywhere from a few days to a few months, but most situations will show improvement within a couple of weeks at most. Only long-standing, chronic habits may take longer to clear up.

If you find that you have trouble remembering to recite your affirmation all day, you can stick little notes all around your house, vehicle and work space to remind you.

You can also choose a piece of jewelry or another item that you can carry with you, and designate it as your "affirmation reminder". Every time you look at or touch the item, it's your cue to state the affirmation a few times.

Another good reminder is to choose a common word like "the" or "and" – and every time you hear or see that word throughout the day, take it as a cue to recite your affirmation.

Within a few days of nearly constant repetition you should have a much easier time remembering, but in the meantime these little "cues" can help a lot.

~ Chapter Five ~
The Best Way to Recite Affirmations

Did you know that there are ways of saying affirmations that make them <u>immensely</u> more powerful? Most people say affirmations flatly, like they are reading a newspaper article. Not surprisingly, they do not achieve great results from affirmations!

Instead, try injecting some of the following into your affirmations:

Passion
Feelings of passion are incredibly uplifting and motivating, and can give a strong boost to your affirmations, helping them sink into your mind much faster.

Notice the difference between these affirmations:

- "I truly love and accept my body."

- **"I TRULY <u>love and accept</u> my body!"**

Can you feel a difference in the emotional impact those two statements have? Needless to say, injecting a strong dose of passion into your affirmations can double, triple, even quadruple their effectiveness – and as a result dramatically increase the results you get from them.

Power

The same thing goes for power. The more empowered you feel when reciting your affirmations, the more effective they are going to be. Notice the difference between the following two affirmations:

- "I am open to the flow of abundance now."

- **"I AM open to the flow of ABUNDANCE NOW."**

This makes the affirmation more like a command than just a positive statement of fact, and it's a great way to get over any feelings of uncertainty or doubt you may have. Just say your affirmation with strength and power in your voice (or even mentally) and you will quickly notice a sense of inner strength and determination rising up within you.

Conviction

Conviction is similar to power but it's more about believing that your affirmation is true, and underlining the fact that you believe it.

- "I am successful at everything I do."

- **"I AM successful at EVERYTHING I do."**

Period. Done. End of story! Can you sense the finality being expressed here? When you say affirmations with a strong sense of conviction, you are asserting that they are the truth, period. This is powerful because you are using your conscious mind to impress a new "truth" into your subconscious mind. Repetition is necessary before it will stick, but it will eventually stick.

Faking It Is Okay!

I should note that it's okay to fake your feelings of passion, power and conviction at first. In fact, you may have to do that if you don't feel very confident when you first start using affirmations. By "faking it" I mean that even though there may be a little voice in the back of your mind saying, "Oh please, you know that's not true" you simply ignore it and act as if your affirmation were true anyway. You know it isn't true but you are choosing to act as if it IS true.

Believe me, you won't be acting for long if you keep up with these techniques – they really work in helping to shift your mindset so you feel much more empowered and optimistic about changing any unsatisfactory circumstances in your life.

<u>Other Ways to Use Affirmations</u>

Besides verbally reciting affirmations hundreds of times a day, you can also have a bit of fun with them, boosting their effectiveness even more.

Here are a few ideas:

Write Them Down

Writing your affirmations is incredibly powerful because you have to spend more time focused on them as opposed to just speaking them aloud or mentally reciting them.

For example, "I am ready to meet the love of my life." Imagine writing this statement over and over again, 40 or 50 times in one sitting. How strongly do you think that affirmation would sink into your mind? Pretty strongly!

Meditate and Visualize Them

Rather than just speaking and writing affirmations, you can spend more time on them by devoting 10 or 15 minutes to seeing them in your mind – that means seeing the words as well as seeing the "pictures" of how your life will change when the affirmation becomes truth.

Paint or Draw Them

Speaking of pictures . . . painting or drawing your affirmations is a great way to add more power to them because you help the messages sink in more easily when you access the creative, non-logical side of your brain. It doesn't matter if you're not a professional artist; your pictures don't have to be perfect. You can even use finger-paints or crayons if you want to! The important thing is to have fun creating them and pour a lot of passion and enthusiasm into the creative process.

Carry Them with You

When you are done writing, drawing or painting your affirmations, carry them with you. Fold them up and stick them in your wallet or purse as a constant reminder of what you are striving toward. Whenever possible, take them out and look at them to reignite your motivation.

How Long Will Affirmations Take to Work?

Believe it or not, if you use the techniques in this guide, it shouldn't take long for you to start seeing positive changes – maybe a month at most, but more likely within a couple of weeks. First, before you see any outer changes you will notice inner changes taking place. You will feel better and notice that you don't have such a hard time believing your affirmations are true. This is a sign that you are starting to change your beliefs!

Shortly afterward is when physical changes will take place, especially as you feel more confident about stepping out of your comfort zone and taking action. There are possible delays that can happen, and we will cover these in the "Challenges in Using Affirmations" chapter next.

~ Chapter Six ~
Common Challenges in Using Affirmations

We've covered a lot of ground on the various techniques you can use to create powerful, effective affirmations, but there are also a few challenges you may encounter along the way.

Challenge #1 – Trying to Accomplish Too Much, Too Fast
Affirmations are extremely helpful in dismantling limiting beliefs and forming more empowering beliefs, but if you try to take on too much at once you will likely end up feeling frustrated and getting nowhere.

This is where the gradual step-up technique we covered comes in handy. Rather than trying to leap straight from a belief that says, "I have no money" to a belief that says, "I am a millionaire" – start smaller.

Remember that many of your existing beliefs are very old, very well-established thought patterns and it may take time to change them. Your odds of success are much greater if you baby-step your way to your goals rather than trying to take one giant leap from here to there.

Challenge #2 – Trying to Believe the Unbelievable
Some affirmations won't work because they are just too unbelievable and you can't wrap your mind around them.

For example, if you currently earn $20,000 per year, you wouldn't want to create an affirmation that says "I earn $1,000,000 per year" because that's just too far outside the realm of your existing reality.

If you tried repeating an affirmation like that, all you would do is trigger limiting beliefs like these: "I could never find a job to pay me that much money. I don't have the education or experience. Only CEOs earn that kind of money."

Instead, try the step-up technique here too. Rather than aiming for a massive goal, try affirming that you can double your current income, or choose a goal that's just slightly larger than your existing reality, like earning an extra $10,000 next year.

You can always keep stepping it up and up and up as you go along!

Challenge #3 – Inconsistent Effort

I said it earlier and I'll say it again; you have to be consistent and proactive with affirmations to make them work! Forming new habits can be difficult, but do whatever you can to be consistent with your efforts.

If you can, set aside some time at the same time each day to work on your affirmations. First thing in the morning, last thing before you go to sleep, during your lunch break – whenever you can fit affirmations in, do them. Be very consistent with it or you will be likely to lose interest because you aren't seeing any results.

Challenge #4 – Expecting Too Much, Too Soon

It would be great if you could say an affirmation a few times and have everything around you transform as if by magic . . . but we both know that's not going to happen. Even if you aren't expecting miracles, it's important to be realistic about just how much you can expect from an affirmation.

Remember that the affirmation itself can only improve your beliefs and make you feel motivated – it will not take the action steps for you.

If you are using affirmations correctly, you should notice that you first start feeling better about the subject, then your belief about it starts shifting to a better place, and then you'll start noticing more and more opportunities that can help you achieve your goal. This happens due to the fact you are becoming more receptive to the opportunities because you are no longer in a closed, pessimistic state of mind.

When opportunities arise, you will know how much the affirmation has improved your state of mind by how willing you are to take action on the opportunities. If you find yourself hanging back, feeling hesitant or anxious, then you still need to keep using the affirmation because you don't yet have a rock-solid belief in it.

Simply keep working at it until you feel that old anxiety fade away, and when the next opportunity comes along, jump at it!

~ Chapter Seven ~
Conclusion: Use Affirmations With Care

I often refer to affirmations as "power tools" because they can transform your life like few other development techniques can. But like all power tools, they must be used correctly to get the intended result. Use them incorrectly and you could end up with results you didn't intend or want – or worse, results that displease you more than your original circumstances did.

One of the greatest things about affirmations is that they can easily be altered and personalized to fit your own goals. If the examples I used in this guide don't resonate with you, keep tweaking them until they do.

Remember that the true power of an affirmation lies in how it makes you feel. If you can feel yourself leaning in a positive direction when you say an affirmation, even if it's a subtle shift, you are on the right track!

Even better, your mastery of using affirmations effectively will continue to grow the more you work with them. You'll be able to "feel" when an affirmation is right for you, and being sure your affirmations are tightly focused like this will allow you to exert less effort but still achieve great results.

In fact, your affirmations will continue to grow and evolve with you. The more work you do on your personal and professional growth, and the more control you gain over your self-talk, the less you will need to do the "stepping-up" technique we described at the beginning of this book. You simply won't feel the need to "soften" your affirmations to make them more believable. Instead, you will easily remain open to big goals and believe they are possible for you.

As your initial affirmations start to come true, be sure to keep expanding them to be bigger and better! Don't settle for just "good" results – keep going after GREAT results in every area of your life. Make long lists of everything you wish to accomplish, and then steadily and surely change the way you think about those areas of your life.

As you change your thoughts, beliefs, feelings, and actions for the better – the circumstances of your life must also change for the better. Once you understand the reliability of this approach, you should find yourself feeling very motivated and inspired because that means virtually ANYTHING is possible for you.

Every goal is achieved the same way; step by step.

~ Chapter Eight ~
Affirmations for the Physical Body

Affirmations for Weight Loss

I choose to be healthy.

I am the perfect weight for me.

I let go of any negative beliefs I have about my body.

I always take care of my body.

I love healthy food.

My mind is focused on losing weight.

I am living a healthy lifestyle.

I love my slim, fit body.

I only eat healthy food.

I am motivated to lose weight.

I am finding it easier to live a healthy lifestyle.

I believe in my ability to lose weight.

I accept and love my body.

I have a naturally slim build.

I find it easy to stay in shape.

I love eating nourishing, healthy food.

I deserve to be healthy and slim.

I deserve to lose weight.

I always think positively about my weight.

I have a naturally healthy body and mind.

I am attracted to healthy food and drink.

I believe in myself and my ability to lose weight.

My body is getting slimmer every day.

I love being thin and healthy.

Losing body fat is easy and effortless for me.

My metabolism increases every day.

I can feel my body becoming slimmer.

It is easy for me to lose weight and keep it off.

My slim body makes me feel confident.

I have a high metabolism and am able to burn fat easily.

My body is a fat burning machine.

I am physically, emotionally and mentally balanced.

I am grateful for my health and physical fitness.

I am becoming more fit and stronger every day.

My body feels light and healthy.

I lose fat quickly and easily.

My energy and vitality increases every day.

My body's cells renew themselves in a healthy way.

I love myself, I love my body.

I feel fantastic in my clothes.

I enjoy exercising several times a week.

I feel sexy and confident.

I have the power to lose weight.

I am willing to change my body.

I find it easy to burn fat.

I love and care for my body.

I deserve to be beautiful.

My body fulfils my every need.

Losing weight comes naturally for me.

I am willing to change my eating habits.

I have a healthy attitude towards foods.

I am physically balanced and healthy.

I am proud of myself and my body.

I allow myself to be healthy and happy.

I love the taste of healthy food.

I look and feel great.

I am in control of how much I eat.

I am responsible for my health.

I am creating a body that is healthy and slim.

I am committed to losing weight.

Affirmations for Anti Aging

The cells in my body grow younger and younger every day.

Every day in every way I am growing younger looking.

I look and feel 10 years younger than I am.

I am full of energy and vitality.

I have youthful skin.

I produce enough collagen to keep my skin young and healthy.

My facial muscles are firm and plump.

I love my youthful appearance.

I maintain a youthful appearance by thinking positive thoughts.

My skin is radiant and wrinkle free.

My body is a beautiful temple.

I am beautiful, happy and confident.

My eyes are bright and clear.

My eyesight is naturally strong and healthy.

I have perfect 20/20 vision.

Every day in every way my eyesight is getting better and better.

I look amazing for my age.

I love having a youthful appearance.

I always receive compliments on how young I look.

My body is healthy and strong.

My organs are healthy and strong.

I am ageless.

I feel young and strong every day.

The cells of my body regenerate in a healthy, youthful way.

I am longevity.

My joints feel strong and healthy.

My hormone levels are balanced.

I feel pretty and sexy.

I am confident in the way I look.

I dissolve all obstacles to having complete self-confidence.

Affirmations for Weight Gain

I nourish my body with healthy foods.

I love and accept my body.

I am willing to make positive changes in my diet.

I am getting closer to reaching my ideal weight of _____.

I find it easy to maintain my weight of _____.

I am full of energy and I feel great.

My body makes me feel confident and sexy.

I am so happy and grateful for my perfect body.

I can overcome any obstacle because I am strong and powerful.

I love and respect myself.

I am grateful for my weight gain.

Even though this feels difficult at times, I am capable of reaching my ideal weight.

I am patient with myself and my body.

I deserve and accept perfect health now.

My mind is positive and focused on gaining weight.

I feel calm and relaxed.

I love life, I love my body and I feel fantastic.

I accept the body of my dreams now.

I am honest and open with myself about my weight gain journey.

I choose to be _____ pounds and I accept it now.

Affirmations for Healthy Hair & Nails

I have healthy, shiny hair.

My hair is growing in a healthy way.

I love my silky, shiny hair.

My hair is easily manageable.

My hair grows longer every day.

Each day my hair becomes silkier and more luscious.

I think beautiful thoughts about my hair and it shows.

People always comment on how beautiful my hair looks.

I am blessed with beautiful, luscious hair.

I am very proud of my hair.

I feel more handsome/attractive every day.

I deserve to look and feel fantastic.

I deserve to have healthy hair and I accept it now.

My hair cells are healthy and strong.

My scalp is healthy and strong.

I have naturally healthy hair.

My hair grows easily and rapidly.

I love taking great care of my hair.

I have soft, silky, luscious hair.

My hair is long, healthy and grows very quickly.

My hairstyle suits my face perfectly.

My scalp is well nourished by healthy blood circulation.

My hair grows more full every day.

I am free from nail biting.

I have the power to control my nail biting.

My nails are naturally strong.

I am in control of my habits.

My fingernails become stronger every day.

My fingernails are a beautiful shape.

I deserve healthy, strong nails and I accept them now.

Affirmations for Exercise

I am willing to accept exercise as part of my daily routine.

Exercise makes me feel healthier and healthier.

My body is becoming more fit every day.

I am naturally motivated to get into shape.

The more I exercise the more motivated I become.

I am totally focused on getting my body in shape.

My body is firm and toned.

I deserve to have a firm and toned body.

I love exercise, it makes me feel exhilarated.

I am finding it easier to motivate myself to exercise.

It feels great when I exercise regularly and look after myself.

Keeping my body healthy and fit is extremely important to me.

I love the feeling I get when I finish my workout.

Being fit and healthy is one of the main priorities in my life.

My body feels more slim and lighter each time I exercise.

Every day my body becomes stronger and leaner.

Every day my body becomes slimmer and more fit.

I am always looking for new fun ways to stay healthy and fit.

I always have a bounce in my step after I exercise.

Exercise energizes my body and revitalizes my mind.

Each time I exercise I build more muscle and burn more fat.

Exercise makes my body feel strong and powerful.

Every day I love exercise more and more.

I always find the time to exercise.

Each time I exercise, I am closer to achieving my ideal weight.

Affirmations for Health

All the organs of my body are functioning perfectly.

Every day in every way I am feeling healthier and healthier.

I am good to my body and my body is good to me.

I love and appreciate my body and treat it accordingly.

I deeply appreciate my healthy body.

I love and accept myself exactly as I am.

I deserve to be healthy and strong.

I love and nurture my body.

I keep my body healthy by having a positive mind.

I love my body and treat it with the respect it deserves.

I send love and appreciation to all the cells of my body.

All the cells of my body multiply in a perfect, healthy way.

My body is a reflection of excellent health.

My body is a temple and I treat it with love and respect.

My muscles and bones are strong and healthy.

My hormone levels are always perfectly balanced.

My lungs and heart are healthy and strong.

My mind is focused on keeping my body at its optimum health.

I practise being healthy every day.

Every cell in my body repairs and replenishes itself with ease.

I send love and gratitude to my healthy organs.

Each and every day moves me towards improved health.

I allow myself to be in good health at all times.

I am blessed with abundant health.

I am healthy, strong, whole and complete.

I am in control of my health at all times.

I choose to be healthy and pain free.

I am living a full, healthy life.

I enjoy perfect health and energy.

My immune system is strong and efficient.

I enjoy a healthy, lifestyle.

I choose abundant health and wellness as my birthright.

I am able to relax my body and calm my mind.

I take excellent care of my body and mind.

I understand and appreciate my body more and more every day.

My body and mind are a reflection of perfect health.

Perfect health vibrates through every cell of my body.

I grow stronger and healthier every day.

I always choose nutritious foods to keep my immune system strong and healthy.

I digest my foods in a healthy and efficient way.

~ Chapter Nine ~
Affirmations for Wealth & Success

Affirmations for Money

I now choose to accept money into my life.

I deserve to be wealthy and I accept wealth now.

Large sums of money come to me in many ways.

My mind is focused on wealth and abundance.

I am attracting money into my life on a daily basis.

I am very lucky when it comes to money.

I love being able to spend money on anything I want.

I trust in the universe to provide me with enough money for all my needs.

I believe there is enough money in the universe for everyone.

I choose to be rich and wealthy.

I understand and respect money.

I manifest wealth in fun and surprising ways.

Every day in every way I am getting wealthier and wealthier.

I feel comfortable about possessing large sums of money.

I feel more and more comfortable around money every day.

My financial security grows every day.

I trust in the good that money can bring.

Financial freedom comes to me easily and effortlessly.

I love being able to spend money on my family and friends.

Having financial abundance enables me to help other people.

My inner child is wealthy and abundant.

I effortlessly attract money into my life.

Everything I touch turns to gold.

I always have more than enough money.

I feel secure knowing that I can afford what I want.

My thoughts about money are always positive.

I regularly come across great financial opportunities.

I believe in my ability to make money.

Having money makes me smile.

I have a positive bank balance at all times.

Every day is a wealthy day.

Being wealthy brings me joy and happiness.

I believe I have the right to be rich.

I am wealthy, I am wealthy, I am wealthy.

I am rich beyond my wildest dreams.

My financial dreams are coming true.

I trust that the universe will always provide me with more money than I need.

I deserve to be prosperous.

I always meet my financial goals.

I allow myself to be wealthy.

I give myself permission to spend money on myself.

I earn more money than I need to spend.

I am a money magnet.

I deserve to have financial freedom.

Money follows me wherever I go.

My wallet is always full of money.

I always attract lucrative situations in my life.

I really enjoy making money.

Having plenty of money is my divine right.

My income is constantly increasing.

Affirmations for Career

I am actively seeking the perfect career for me.

I accept new career opportunities now.

I deserve to have a successful career.

I am now attracting the perfect career to match my talents.

My new job brings joy and satisfaction into my life.

The universe is manifesting my ideal job and I accept it now.

Fantastic career opportunities present themselves to me.

My ideal job is coming to me right now.

I am incredibly fulfilled in my career.

My job offers me complete creative freedom.

I have an excellent relationship with my work colleagues.

Every day in every way my career is getting more successful.

My job has fantastic perks.

My career is growing in leaps and bounds.

I now have a wonderful job that I love.

I always make a great impression at any interview I attend.

I have the greatest job in the world for me.

I always find job hunting easy and successful.

I have a rewarding job that pays me very well.

I always make the best career choices for me.

I am confident that my ideal job is just around the corner.

I am so happy and grateful for my successful career.

I work the right amount of hours to suit my needs.

I have an exciting and enjoyable career.

Affirmations for Success

I am now attracting success in my life.

Every day in every way I am becoming more and more successful.

Success follows me wherever I go.

My life is filled with success after success.

I deserve to be successful and I accept it now.

I have a wonderful, successful life.

I am worthy of success.

I am wealthy and successful.

I have a successful attitude towards life.

I have positive beliefs about success.

I attract success into my life.

I choose to be successful.

Success is my birthright and I manifest it now.

My success makes me feel happy and content.

I am a success magnet.

My mind is focused on attracting success into my life.

Every day brings more success into my life.

My relationships are a success.

Everything I do brings me even more success.

I always achieve everything I set out to do.

I am surrounded by successful, positive people.

I am a winner, I am successful.

I know that I have what it takes to be a great success.

I have the power to succeed in whatever I do.

I am very capable of success.

My business grows more successful every day.

I am successfully achieving all of my goals.

Success is drawn to me every day.

I am confident in my ability to be successful.

I am the owner of a very successful business.

I give thanks for the abundant success in my life.

Whatever I focus my mind on, I achieve.

Success follows me wherever I go.

My energy radiates success and prosperity.

I know my future will be successful.

I always make the right choices in my life.

I expect success and it flows into my life easily.

I feel successful and confident.

I am the secret to my success.

The universe guides me from one successful situation to another.

Affirmations for Abundance

A constant stream of abundance flows towards me.

Every day I discover new ways to become more abundant.

I give thanks for the abundance in my life every day.

Abundance flows into my life easily and effortlessly.

Every day in every way I am feeling more abundant.

I accept the flow of abundance into my life.

My mind is focused on abundance and that is what I attract every day.

I am a powerful abundance magnet.

I allow abundance to flow freely in all areas of my life.

The universe supplies exactly what I need, whenever I need it.

I deserve abundance in my life and I accept it now.

I bless the limitless abundance in my life.

I have an infinite supply of abundance in every aspect of my life.

My abundance is constantly increasing.

There is a continuous stream of abundance flowing into my life.

The universe is abundant and has enough for everyone.

I claim my right to be abundant.

My life is overflowing with abundance and prosperity.

It is ok for me to be abundant.

I rejoice in the prospect of unlimited abundance and prosperity.

I live in a rich and abundant universe.

I have a positive attitude towards abundance.

Abundance comes to me in more ways than I can imagine.

My belief in abundance grows on a daily basis.

I am worthy of receiving abundance.

I give myself permission to enjoy the abundance in my life.

I am creating more and more of what I want every day in effortless ways.

I am creating more experiences that generate feelings of joy.

I am open to receiving an abundance of wealth, health and happiness.

I love the exciting opportunities of wealth and abundance that come my way.

~ Chapter Ten ~
Affirmations for Love & Relationships

Affirmations for Love

I am in a loving, supportive relationship.

I attract only healthy, loving people into my life.

I am surrounded by loving, harmonious relationships.

I am worthy of being loved.

Love is flowing to me and through me at all times.

I love and accept myself exactly the way I am.

I allow myself to be loved fully.

I am a magnet for my loving, perfect match.

I have a harmonious, loving relationship with my partner.

I only attract positive people into my life.

My life is filled with love and happiness.

I welcome love with open arms.

I choose to accept love in my life.

I deserve to be treated with love and respect.

I am loving, kind and a wonderful person.

I am always connected to my highest good.

The universe surrounds me with love.

My heart is always open and I radiate love.

Everywhere I go, I discover love and it feels amazing.

I radiate love and it is returned to me multiplied.

I love and trust in myself to make the right choices in life.

The more love I give the more there is to receive.

I see love in everybody around me.

I am always present and in the moment.

My world is filled with love, light and happiness.

I share my love with others.

I love openly, unconditionally, honestly and compassionately.

Love and miracles surround me everywhere I go.

I celebrate love and life every day.

I am a love magnet.

I am attracting my perfect partner to me right now.

I am ready to welcome a loving relationship into my life now.

I welcome love and love welcomes me.

I am a magnificent being with an abundance of love to give.

I am cherished and valued.

I am greeted by love wherever I go.

I am loving and compassionate to myself and others.

I am willing to move myself unconditionally.

I choose to be loving and accepting of people.

Love is a beautiful gift from the universe.

Affirmations for Friendship

I am making new friends easily.

I am a warm, friendly person and people like me.

I attract like-minded people into my life.

I am creating lasting friendships in my life.

I cherish my friends.

I am attracting magnificent life-long friends into my life.

I have close friends who support me and make me laugh.

I always find it easy to have fun with my friends.

I find it easy to talk to people.

I have lasting friendships with wonderful, caring people.

I have an abundance of loving, like-minded friends.

I attract beautiful friendships into my life.

My friends and I have so much fun together.

I am so grateful for my friends and love them dearly.

My wonderful friends are supportive, kind, trustworthy and loyal.

My friends allow me the freedom to be the person I truly am.

All my friendships are harmonious and empowering.

Everyone I meet accepts me for the wonderful person I am.

I always make time to spend with my friends.

I am a devoted and loyal friend.

My close friends are a very important part of my life.

I am always attracting loyal and friendly people into my life.

I love meeting new people.

I am now willing to accept happy, fulfilling relationships.

I attract genuine friendships into my life.

I can always rely on my friends.

It is ok to be myself around my friends.

I connect easily with others.

I find it incredibly easy to make new friends.

I have a wonderful circle of friends who love and appreciate me.

I have a lot of friends who share my interests.

I have the greatest respect and admiration for my friends.

I help people feel at ease.

I am a great listener.

I love laughing and having fun with my friends.

My friends and I always make each other laugh.

I love socializing with my friends.

I love my close friends unconditionally.

I naturally attract positive friendships into my life.

My friends encourage me in everything I do.

Affirmations for Romance

I attract romance in the most magical and unexpected ways.

My partner is romantic, thoughtful and understanding to my needs.

My relationship with _____ is growing more romantic and harmonious every day.

Romance is a beautiful gift in my life.

I love being romantic with _____.

Romance finds me wherever I go.

I love having romantic nights out with _____.

My partner always finds a reason to be romantic towards me.

_____ and I have my perfect romantic relationship.

My partner and I are free to express our feelings towards each other.

My partner always finds little ways to be romantic every day.

The universe is manifesting romance into my life now.

I am open and ready to receive romance into my life.

My mind is focused on a romantic relationship.

I radiate romantic energy.

Passion, romance and love are flowing into my life.

I find it easy to manifest romance into my life.

I choose to have a romantic relationship with my partner.

I now believe that relationships can be joyful and romantic.

Romance and love flow to me easily and effortlessly.

I rejoice in the romance I encounter every day.

I deserve to have a romantic, loving relationship.

I trust the universe to know the type of partner who is perfect for me.

I know that I deserve romance and I accept it now.

My natural romantic nature attracts romance to me like a magnet.

I am in a joyous intimate relationship with a person who truly loves me.

I deserve love and romance and I get them in abundance.

I am worthy of love and romance.

Our relationship is charged with the energy of love and romance.

Romance and sensuality are natural feelings in my relationship.

Affirmations for Family

My parents accept and love me for who I am.

My parents express their love for me in the best way they know how.

I understand my parents have a past and are doing the best they know how.

My siblings and I support and love each other.

I am a member of a loving, supportive family.

I know my family are there for me if I ever need them.

I receive unconditional love from my family.

I always experience positive situations with my family.

My brother/sister and I are taking the time to build on our relationship.

I deserve to have a happy family life and I accept it now.

My family allow me the freedom to be the person I want to be.

My family always encourage and support me.

I am so grateful for the lessons my parents have taught me.

My family and I always make time for one another.

Every day I give thanks for my wonderful family.

Everyone in my family is healthy and happy.

I always look forward to spending quality time with my family.

I am considerate of my family's feelings.

I am very close to my family.

My family demonstrate their love for me in infinite ways, as I do them.

I really enjoy family get-togethers and the fun we have.

I am so proud to belong to my lovely family.

I listen carefully when a member of my family needs me.

I have an infinite amount of patience with my family.

I have made peace with my mother/father.

I help my family whenever I can.

I love bringing joy and happiness into the lives of my family.

I love my family with all my heart.

I only think loving, positive thoughts about my family.

I show compassion and empathy to each member of my family.

Affirmations for Parent/Children

I am a patient and understanding parent.

I am a responsible and kind parent.

I am a great Mom/Dad.

I always act responsibly around my children.

I am sensitive towards my families' needs.

I am so grateful for my beautiful, healthy children.

I have a loving relationship with my children.

I am very proud of my children.

I am open and affectionate with my children.

I understand my children's needs.

I allow my children to grow up and be their own person.

I give all my children equal amounts of my time.

I do everything possible to encourage my children to reach their goals.

I encourage any talent my child displays.

I teach my children manners and respect.

I praise my children every day for the wonderful people they are.

I have total confidence in my ability as a parent.

I have complete confidence in my ability to raise happy children.

I have a positive influence on my children.

I create a happy, loving home for my children to grow up in.

I help my children whenever they ask.

I always include my children in any important family decisions.

I inspire my children to be the best they can be.

I love creating fun and laughter with my children.

I instil positive beliefs in my children.

I encourage my children to be positive and optimistic.

My partner and I always agree on what is best for our children.

I enjoy a peaceful, harmonious life with my children.

My family always come first in my life.

My children and I always communicate with each other.

I teach my children to always be respectful to others.

I take an active interest in my children's education.

My children and I enjoy each other's company.

I strive to be the best parent I can be.

I love spending quality time with my children.

I send light and love to my children every day.

I am empowered by the love I receive from my children.

Every day in every way my relationship with my children is getting better and better.

I have a very strong bond with my children.

My children enrich my life in magical ways.

Affirmations for Marriage

I am excited about marriage and am ready for it now.

I am open to marriage and I am attracting my perfect partner now.

I am divinely guided in my search for my perfect partner.

I believe in the sanctity of marriage.

I am in a happy, harmonious marriage.

_____ & I respect our marriage and each other.

My partner and I are extremely happy in our marriage.

My marriage is a joyous union of love and laughter.

I love and deeply appreciate my marriage.

I am devoted to my spouse.

I adore being married.

Every day in every way our marriage is growing stronger and stronger.

I am in a loyal, trustworthy marriage.

My marriage is sacred to me and I cherish every minute of it.

My wedding day was the best day of my life.

I am planning the most beautiful, fabulous wedding.

I enable my husband/wife to enjoy his/her freedom when he/she needs it.

My husband/wife and I are open and sharing with each other.

My marriage brings me infinite joy and happiness.

I am confident in my marriage.

My husband/wife and I communicate in a calm, healthy way.

My husband/wife and I have an equal say in making decisions in our lives.

I believe in my partner, he/she is a wonderful person.

My husband/wife and I understand each other's needs.

I pay attention to my spouse's needs.

I always focus on the positive things in my marriage.

I always appreciate the little things my husband/wife does.

I love my spouse with all my heart.

We love each other just the way we are.

Our marriage is healthy and happy.

My marriage grows more passionate every day.

I always speak to my spouse with the utmost respect.

My husband/wife and I have a very healthy sex life.

I love spending time with my spouse.

My husband/wife and I always make time for each other.

I am a loving, faithful wife/husband.

I am blissfully married.

I am immensely grateful for my marriage.

My marriage is filled with laughter and fun times.

I am passionate about keeping my marriage alive and exciting.

I am committed to making my marriage work.

I appreciate my partner's romantic, thoughtful gestures and return the same.

I fully support my husband/wife's career.

I have now found my perfect partner.

I love showing my wife/husband how much I love them.

I trust my partner completely.

It still feels like love at first sight when I look at my husband/wife.

My husband/wife is my best friend.

I express my love for my husband/wife on a regular basis and it is returned to me multiplied.

My husband/wife and I bring out the best in each other.

~ Chapter Eleven ~
Affirmations for Self Image

Affirmations for Self Esteem

I recognize the many good qualities I have.

I am feeling happier with myself more and more every day.

I am a good person.

I choose to see myself in a positive light.

I surround myself with people who bring out the best in me.

I am becoming a better person every day.

I believe in myself.

I love and respect myself.

I deserve all that is good.

I release all negative self talk and only focus on the positive.

I am grateful for being given the gift of life.

I now believe I have the power to change my life.

I can change.

I am a magnificent person.

I am able to express my feelings with others.

I feel good about being me.

It is ok to be me.

Amazing opportunities exist for me in every area of my life.

I am beginning to feel better about myself a little each day.

I now realize that I am a wonderful person.

I am courageous and strong.

I have the ability to attract and create positive situations in my life.

I am a beautiful human being.

I feel a divine sense of self worth, an abundance of positive energy and a high level of self esteem.

I am capable, confident and smart.

I love the person I am becoming more and more every day.

I know that I have good qualities and I recognize them in myself more with each passing day.

I care about myself and others.

I approve of myself more each day.

I value my mind, body and spirit.

Affirmations for Confidence

I am confident in my ability to create a positive future for myself.

I love change and can adjust easily to new situations.

I am confident, strong and powerful.

I am a good communicator.

My personality exudes confidence.

I have a confident mind.

I always express my thoughts and feelings with confidence.

I am outgoing and confident in social situations.

My confidence in myself is growing stronger every day.

Every day in every way I am becoming more and more confident.

I believe in myself and my ability to succeed.

I am confident in my ability to progress in life.

I am a naturally confident person.

My confidence improves with each passing day.

My increasing confidence improves my life in magical ways.

I enjoy being confident, it lifts my spirit and makes me feel good.

I pursue each of my goals with absolute confidence.

I trust in myself and have total faith in my abilities.

I move forward with courage and conviction.

My thoughts and opinions are valuable.

I have strong beliefs about myself.

I appreciate my self confidence.

I express myself with confidence.

I am beautiful inside and out.

I release the need to judge or criticize myself.

I am in control of my thoughts and emotions.

I feel great about myself and my life.

I know I can achieve anything.

I feel good about my future.

I walk tall.

Affirmations for Strength

I have the strength and determination to get me to the place I deserve to be.

My strength grows stronger every day.

The universe gives me the strength to pursue my dreams.

I am a strong, powerful person.

I have the courage and strength to manifest the life of my dreams.

I have more than enough strength to achieve my goals.

I am a tower of strength and courage.

My past experiences have made me the strong person I am today.

I am a focused and determined individual.

I can face any situation that comes my way.

I have fantastic willpower and determination.

I am in control of my life.

I trust in my inner strength.

My inner strength grows stronger every day.

I am prepared to take on any challenge, knowing I will be successful in everything I do.

I am a strong, capable person, capable of achieving great things.

I am ready to use my talents to create positive changes in my life.

I have the strength to stand my ground and make my own decisions.

I release any fear of failure.

I summon up the courage and strength to face my fears.

I am strong enough to be myself.

I give and receive strength every day.

I feel the strongest I have felt in a long time.

It's ok to have strong opinions and to voice them.

I feel emotionally and mentally strong.

I have great moral courage and strength.

I breathe in strength and courage.

I have the power to create feelings of joy, happiness and abundance.

I manifest perfect health and strength.

I focus on my inner strength and power.

Affirmations for Wisdom

My wisdom is a gift from God.

My intuition is increased because of my wisdom.

I am where I am supposed to be.

My life is guided by the divine principle.

My inner self always knows what path to take.

I open my heart to the wisdom and love of the universe.

I trust my inner wisdom.

I am wise and intelligent.

Divine wisdom flows freely into my life.

I am divinely guided in everything I do.

I possess infinite intelligence and I use it wisely.

I radiate wisdom and understanding.

I can face any challenge in life knowing that I have infinite wisdom.

I am centered and connected to my higher self.

I relax and allow my inner wisdom to radiate from me.

I am connected to source energy.

I trust my intuitive voice.

I allow universal wisdom to flow to me.

Every day in every way my intuition grows stronger and stronger.

I am one with myself.

Affirmations for Attitude

I have a positive attitude towards life.

I can take on anything, I am a winner.

My positive attitude creates magical experiences in my life.

I am unstoppable.

I feel fantastic today.

I wake up every morning with positivity and gratitude for my wonderful life.

I have an easy going attitude about life.

I focus my attitude on the beauty and joy of life.

I live my life to the fullest.

I love sharing my positive attitude with others.

I maintain a positive attitude every day.

I always see the best in people.

I am feeling on top of the world.

I have what it takes to be the best.

My positive attitude enables me to always reach my goals.

My positive attitude is reflected in my healthy, energetic body.

Today is the best day, I feel wonderful.

My positive attitude brings great joy and success into my life.

I have the passion and drive to make my dreams a reality.

I always expect the best and that is exactly what I get.

Affirmations for Memory

I always remember people's names with ease.

I have a masterful memory.

I am able to recall any information I need.

I love and respect my brain and the wonderful job it does every day.

I am able to easily remember small details.

My memory is getting better every day.

I am so grateful for my fantastic memory.

I easily recall the events of my past.

I completely trust my memory to provide information when I need it.

I have a photographic memory when it comes to books I read.

I always remember my dreams in clear detail.

I have an excellent memory for numbers.

I find it incredibly easy to remember people's faces.

I remember facts easily.

My memory is improving with every passing day.

My ability to remember past experiences improves every day.

I recall information easily and effortlessly.

I remember everything I learn in college/university.

I love exercising my memory.

I retrieve information from memory with total ease.

~ Chapter Twelve ~
Affirmations for Peace & Harmony

Affirmations for Forgiveness

Each day I learn to forgive myself a little more.

The more I learn to forgive myself, the more I learn to forgive others.

I am forgiving, understanding and compassionate.

Today is the first day of the rest of my life.

I let go of past grievances and forgive freely.

I recognize the need to forgive others.

I am willing to start forgiving people from my past.

I forgive others and move on with my life.

I radiate forgiveness and set myself free.

I forgive my inner child.

I forgive my family and surround them with love and compassion.

By forgiving myself and others I set myself free.

I choose forgiveness now.

I take back my freedom by forgiving myself and others.

I am dissolving all obstacles to achieving my goals.

I am excited about moving forward in my life.

I choose to feel compassion and empathy towards others.

I choose to let go of the past and embrace the future.

I forgive others and they forgive me.

I am willing to take the next step towards a better future.

I am willing to let go of my past and forgive.

I forgive my parents and understand they did the best they could.

I release all negative memories and move on.

I empower my subconscious with positive beliefs.

I am willing to let go and experience joy in my life.

I choose to release all sadness from my past and focus on the happy memories I have.

I forgive the past and welcome the present.

I forgive myself for any negative self talk or negative self beliefs I had.

I forgive myself for any unkind thing I did in the past.

I forgive myself for not being perfect.

I freely release the need to be perfect.

I heal my pain by releasing past grievances.

I trust in the universe to guide me on my path to forgiveness.

I let go of any past conflicts in my life and move forward with love.

I lovingly release myself from my past.

I compassionately release my fear of forgiveness.

I release all negative energy from my body and mind.

I am ready to release any negative memories from my mind.

I release any resentment I feel towards _____ and send him/her love and happiness.

I release the past and live in the now.

Affirmations for Happiness

I attract happiness into my life.

Happiness follows me wherever I go.

I choose to be happy now.

I wake up each morning and choose to be happy.

I am brimming with happiness and positivity.

I radiate happiness, joy and beauty.

Feeling happy is my divine right.

I put myself in situations that make me feel happy.

I deserve to be happy.

It is ok to be happy.

All aspects of my life are happy and joyful.

Thinking happy, positive thoughts attract happy positive experiences in my life.

I love feeling happy.

I have an optimistic outlook on life.

My soul resonates with joy and happiness.

I become more happy every day.

I am surrounded by happy optimistic people.

Every day brings me great joy.

I choose to follow my bliss.

I am a happy go-lucky person.

I always make time to experience joy.

I always smile at people and act in a friendly manner.

I am happy and content with my life.

I am happy and grateful for everything I have in my life.

I am happy and grateful for every person in my life.

I choose to spread happiness wherever I go.

I am ready to have a happy perspective on life.

I am very happy to be me.

Happiness is there for the taking.

I embrace happiness with love and gratitude.

Happiness is my birthright and I accept it now.

I enjoy laughing and having fun.

I choose to create a life filled with joy and happiness.

I feel happy and content as I go about my day.

I find joy and happiness in the simple things in life.

I always try to make other people happy.

I always find reasons to be happy.

I know that happiness is a choice and I practice it every day.

I acknowledge that true happiness comes from within.

I love sharing my joy and happiness with others.

Affirmations for Faith

My faith is strong and powerful.

My faith moves mountains.

I have faith in myself and in my abilities.

I am faithful to myself and others.

I have the utmost faith that the universe guides me on the road to success and happiness.

By recognizing the divine in others, I find it easy to recognize it in myself.

My strong faith brings me constant peace and joy.

I have faith in God and all the love that he brings.

I am connected to my inner spirit.

My faith empowers me to be a better person.

I am a child of the universe.

I am a spiritual being radiating light and love.

I am connected to my higher self at all times.

I have faith in mankind.

I am divinely guided by the universe every day.

I am one with my inner child.

I am connected with my eternal spirit at all times.

My faith in all that is good is growing stronger every day.

My guardian angel is always by my side.

My mind and spirit are one.

Affirmations for Peace

I feel divine well-being and peace flow through my body.

I choose peace and calm.

People feel peaceful and calm around me.

I have a calm, relaxed personality.

I act in a calm and peaceful way in any situation.

I am a channel for peace and serenity.

I make time for meditation every day.

I let go of any worry and trust that everything will be ok.

I choose to feel peaceful and at ease.

I have a peaceful home environment.

I radiate peace and love out to others and it comes back to me multiplied.

I live in the present moment and enjoy it completely.

I trust in the process of life.

I am at peace.

Feelings of peace and tranquillity radiate through my body.

I feel calm and relaxed.

All my muscles are becoming more and more relaxed.

My mind is quiet and peaceful.

I inhale peace and harmony and exhale any tension in my body.

Feelings of calm and relaxation energize my body.

With every passing day I am feeling calmer and calmer.

My inner child is centered and at peace.

I am at peace with all my family and friends.

I allow myself to feel calm and relaxed.

A peaceful feeling washes over me.

I find time every day to quiet my mind.

I am beginning to feel more peaceful with each passing day.

I allow peace and serenity to exist in all areas of my life.

I am at peace with my past.

I remain calm and composed in all situations.

I am cool, calm and collected.

I am in complete harmony with my surroundings.

My peaceful mind is a reflection of my clutter-free, organized home.

I feel relaxed and energized every day.

I choose to accept a calmer, more relaxed approach to life.

I feel tranquil, calm and totally relaxed.

I can easily relax my mind and body.

I choose to feel happy and relaxed throughout my day.

I feel more content every day.

I am blessed with peace of mind.

Peace and harmony surround and protect me.

My body feels completely at ease.

I instil feelings of calm in others.

My life is blessed with peace and serenity.

My mind is filled with peaceful thoughts.

Affirmations for Safety

I now choose to feel safe and secure.

I trust in the universe to guide me to safety.

I feel divinely protected in the world.

I am safe and secure at all times.

Feeling safe is my birthright and I accept it now.

I choose to feel safe and secure at all times.

I feel safe and protected at all times.

I surround myself with feelings of safety and security.

My family and home are safe and protected.

My spirit and faith protect me and keep me safe.

Anywhere I go I always feel safe and secure.

I live in a safe, secure neighborhood.

My inner child feels safe and secure.

I see myself safely traveling to and from work every day.

It is safe to be myself.

I always feel safe when I use public transport.

I deserve to feel safe and secure.

It is safe to express my opinions to others.

All of life loves and supports me and makes me feel safe.

The world is a safe place to be.

Affirmations for Trust

All is well in my world.

I trust in the miracle of life.

I let go and trust in the universe.

I trust in the power of love to heal my body.

I trust my intuition.

I trust in the universe to bring the correct people into my life.

I trust in all that is.

I choose to trust other people.

I trust my partner and release any feelings of jealousy.

I trust that everything is going to be ok.

My inner child always leads me in the right direction.

I have a trusting, loving nature.

I have loyal, trusting friends.

I possess the ability to trust and to be trusted.

I trust in the process of life.

My trusting nature is reciprocated by everybody in my life.

I am a naturally trusting person.

I am becoming more and more trusting every day.

My trusting nature makes me feel free and alive.

I give myself permission to trust others.

Affirmations for Life

I love life and all the joy it brings.

I thank God for giving me the precious gift of life.

I accept that life can be filled with happiness and joy.

My life is filled with positive situations.

Every moment in my life is filled with great joy.

Every day in every way my life is getting better and better.

Every day my life becomes more fun.

I am high on life.

I cherish my wonderful life.

I now choose to believe that my life can get better.

I embrace life.

My life is a joyous adventure.

My life is one happy situation after another.

My life is full of joyful surprises.

Abundant joy blesses my life every day.

I choose to change my thoughts.

I choose to create a happy life for myself.

Life is meant to be easy and I accept it now.

I live life to the full.

I love being me.

I am beginning to live my life to the fullest.

I love life and life loves me.

Life always deals me an easy hand and I always choose to accept it.

I recognize that my life has true meaning.

I have the deepest respect and love for life.

The universe blesses my life with miracles every day.

I am so grateful to my parents for giving me the gift of life.

I deliberately create a happy life for myself.

I am manifesting the life of my dreams.

My life is filled with positive, successful, happy people.

53577136R00056

Made in the USA
Lexington, KY
10 July 2016